Habitats

by Jim Pipe

F

Contents

THIS EDITION:
King's Lynn
Norfolk PE30 4HG
Printed in Malaysia
A CIP record for this book is available from the British Library.

FIRST EDITION:
PO Box 53987
London SW15 2SF

DESIGNED BY
Ian McMullen

EDITED BY
Grace Jones

ISBN: 978-1-910512-31-9

ADVISORY TEAM:
Andrea Bright — Science Coordinator, Trafalgar Junior School
Literacy Consultant. Jackie Holderness — former Senior Lecturer in Primary Education, Westminster Institute, Oxford Brookes University. Series Consultants — Anne Fussell — Early Years Teacher and University Tutor, Westminster Institute, Oxford Brookes University. David Fussell — C.Chem., FRSC.

Habitats

A home is a place where we can eat, drink, sleep, work and play. Animals and plants need homes too.

They need a place where there is food, water, shelter and space to live in. This place is called a habitat.

Some habitats are huge areas like deserts, mountains or the sea.

Habitats can be big or small. They can be wet or dry, hot or cold, bright or dark.

Local habitats are woods, ponds, rivers, meadows and the seashore.

Small places like a patch of grass or a windowbox are habitats too.

Living Things

Look at this woodland scene. What living things can you spot?

All living things need a habitat to live in. Plants and animals usually share a habitat with other living things.

Not all living things are plants or animals. Mushrooms are living things called fungi.

Where would you expect to find a woodlouse, worm, snail, butterfly or frog?

In a river, some plants grow underwater.

Trees and bushes live on the river bank. Fish live underwater, but birds and insects live on it.

Deer and mice live on land near the river.

A habitat provides living things with food and water. Plants make food from sunlight and from minerals in the soil. Plants are food for many animals from caterpillars to elephants! Plant-eating animals are often eaten by other animals, called predators. The animals that predators eat are their prey.

A food chain shows what living things eat in a habitat. The arrows go from one living thing to the living thing that eats it.

Can you draw a food chain showing that zebras eat grass and lions eat zebras?

Exploring Habitats

Always take a grown-up when you go exploring.

We share habitats with other animals and plants. If you want to explore a habitat, remember that it is their home too.

Try to watch animals without disturbing them. If you touch pond water or soil, remember to wash your hands afterwards.

Some kestrels hunt in towns and cities. They have changed, or adapted, to a new habitat. What other animals have adapted to life in towns?

Most kinds of plants and animals have lived in the same habitat for thousands of years.

Their body suits the habitat they live in. If we damage a habitat, the animals in it may not be able to live anywhere else.

Trees & Woods

One tree can be a habitat for thousands of living things.

Centipedes hunt slugs and worms in the rotting leaves at the base of a tree. Weevils and beetles feed on tree bark. Bugs and caterpillars nibble new leaves.

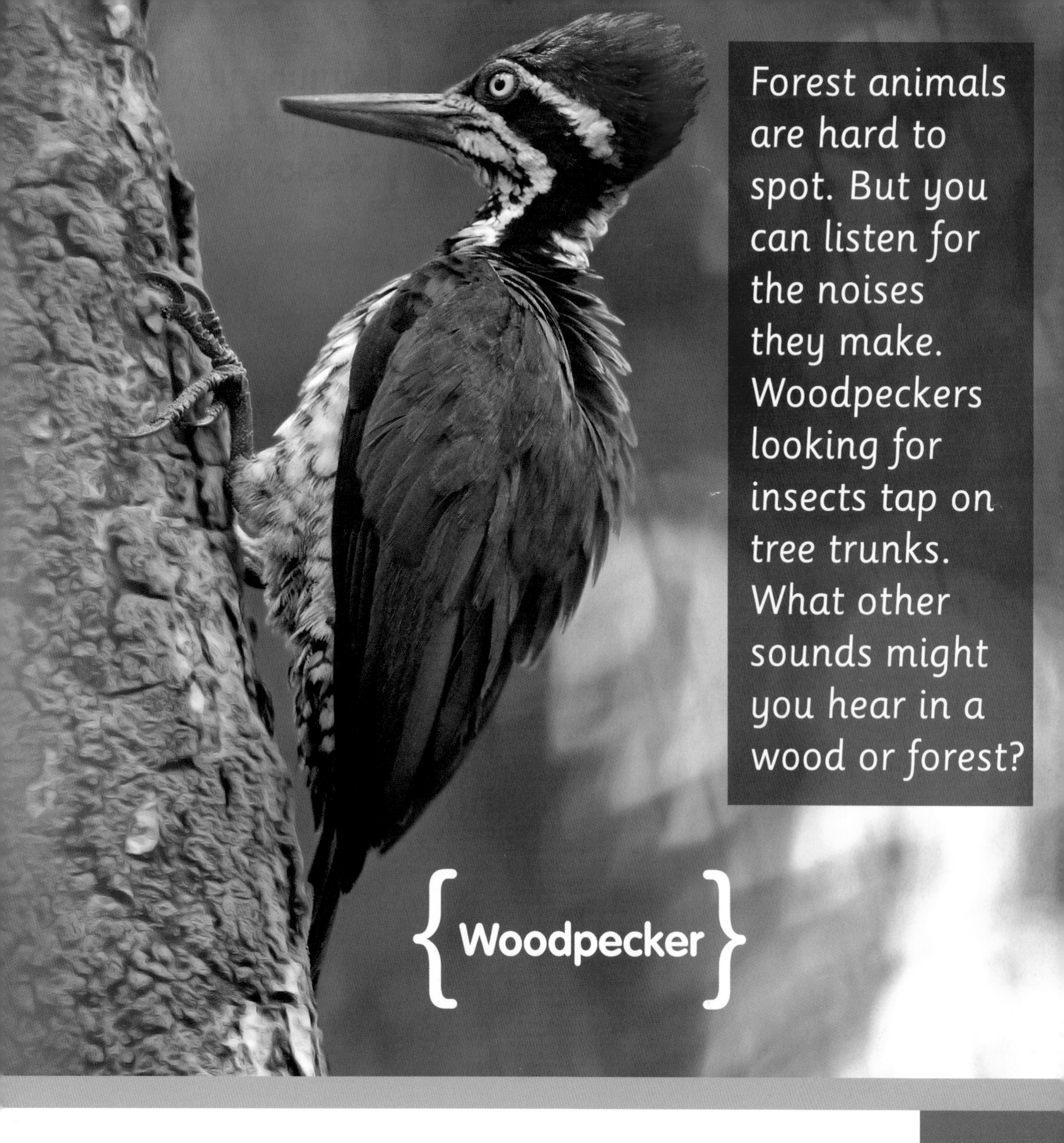

Trees grow together to form woods and forests – habitats for all sorts of animals. Birds and squirrels make their nests in trees. They eat nuts, berries and the minibeasts that live on trees. Larger animals, such as deer and badgers live on the forest floor.

Meadows

When a field is left uncut it grows into a meadow of tall grasses and wild flowers.

Many flowers live in a meadow, such as thistles, buttercups, poppies and foxgloves. Their bright colours attract insects such as bees, wasps and butterflies.

Birds, such as skylarks and blackbirds visit meadows to eat seeds, worms and insects.

Mammals, such as mice and rabbits make their homes in holes underground.

Foxes and owls hunt them at night.

Ponds & Rivers

Many animals live in and around ponds and rivers. Insects, turtles and fish feed on plants that live underwater.

Insects such as whirligigs and pond skaters live on the surface of the water. Dragonflies and frogs hunt flies that live in the air above a pond.

This girl is pond dipping. She uses a jar to collect water from a river. She uses a magnifying glass to spot small animals in the water. What might she find?

Unlike a pond, the water in a river is always moving. Ducks and swans live on the water. They eat plants and insects. They build nests on the river bank.

Kingfishers and otters live on river banks. They hunt for fish under the water.

The Seashore

The seashore is home to many unusual plants and animals. On a sandy beach, clams and other shellfish bury themselves in the sand. Crabs scuttle across the beach, using their large claws to grab prey. Higher up the beach, long grasses live in the sand dunes.

The sea moves up and down the beach twice a day. This is called the tide. When is a good time to look for seashells?

Seaweed

On a rocky beach, pools are left behind when the tide goes out. Plants called seaweed cling to rocks.

Limpets feed on the seaweed and in turn are prey for starfish. Small fish and crabs hunt prawns hiding in the seaweed.

Town Wildlife

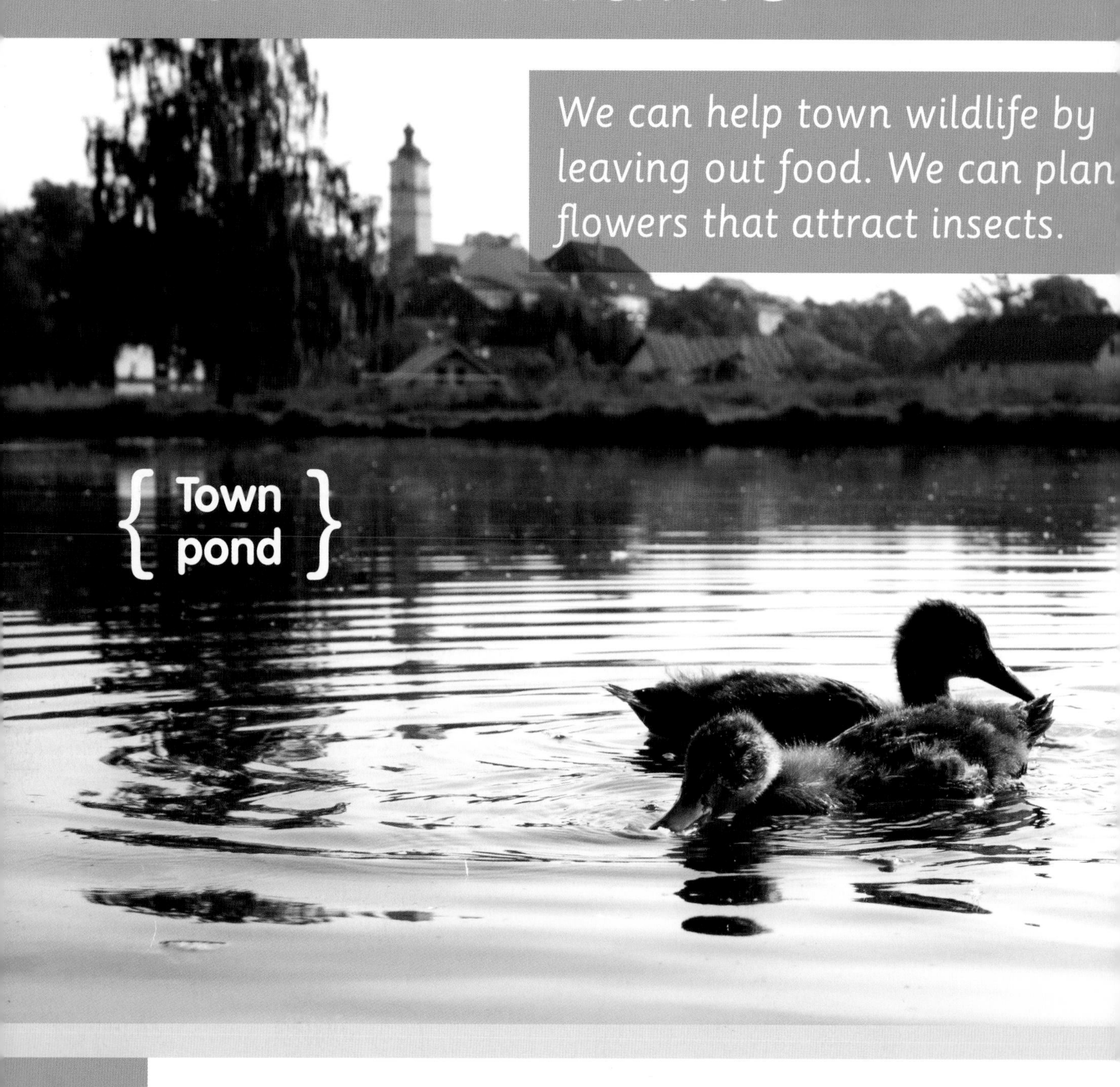

Many animals have learned to live in a town or city habitat.

The trees and bushes in parks provide food and shelter for insects, birds, squirrels and even deer. At night, foxes hunt for food in city dustbins.

Some animals live on us, such as fleas, nits and ticks!

Some animals help to keep our home clean. Spiders eat flies which spread germs. What other animals can you spot inside your home?

Town houses are a habitat for all sorts of birds. Pigeons nest on high buildings.

Sparrows nest under roofs. Mice and rats can live inside walls or under floors. Minibeasts such as moths, cockroaches, ants and beetles can live inside your house.

Habitats in Danger

Some habitats are in danger. When people cut down forests or turn meadows into farms, they kill wild plants. They also destroy animal homes. Some animals die straight away. Others try to move to a new home. The new home may not have enough food and shelter for extra animals.

We can also create new habitats.

We can let an area of grass grow long to create a meadow. We can plant a tree. One day it will be a home to lots of animals. We can build a pond to make a home for water creatures.

Seaside Explorers

Look out for words and ideas about habitats and living things.

It was a lovely spring day. Dan and James were feeling bored in the house, so Dad took them to the beach.

"It's a bit cold to go swimming," said Dan.
"Yes, but look at all that sand," said James.
"Let's go exploring!"

"A beach is a home for lots of living things," said Dad. "Let's see how many we can find."
"There are lots of different places to look," said Dan.
"On the way here I saw seagulls on the cliffs."

"I hope we see dolphins,"
said James.
"Let's climb up to the sand dunes.
We can see far out to sea from
there."
"I can see some animals," said Dan.
"That family is having
a picnic in the long
grass!"

"Do you think they're
wild?" joked James.

The boys looked for
rabbits in the dunes.
"They may be hiding underground in their
burrows," said Dad. "Lots of predators like
to eat rabbits!"

"I've found a paw print!"
shouted James.
"It looks like a dog's
paw," said Dan.
"I saw a woman
walking her dog
along the beach!"

The boys walked towards the sea. Below the dunes was a line of seaweed and shells.
"Look how far the tide comes in," said Dan.
"What's this long shell?" asked James.
"It's a razor-shell," said Dad. "It's the shell from an animal that burrows into the sand."

Further along the beach, Dan found a starfish.
"I hope the tide comes in soon and washes it back to sea."

The boys explored the beach for two more hours. But they found only shells and seaweed.
"Don't worry," said Dad.
"I know a rocky beach we can go to tomorrow."

The next day, Dan spotted some familiar faces when they arrived at the rocky beach.
"It's that family from the sand dunes."
"The girl is collecting shells on the beach," said Dad.
"Maybe she knows a good place to look for animals."

Paula lived near the beach and knew it well. She showed the boys some different types of seaweed. Then they walked over to the rockpools.
"Watch out," said Paula.
"These rocks are very slippery."

All around the rockpool, limpets and periwinkles clung to the rocks.

"Some people scrape limpets off the rocks," said Paula.

"But they're food for many crabs and starfish."

Paula pointed out some sea anemones.

"They look pretty, but they are deadly predators," she said. "They attack prey with their poison tentacles."

"There's a little fish in the rocks. Will the anemone get it?" asked Dan.

"Phew! It got away this time."

Something else was moving under the water.
It was a hermit crab.
"You can pick it up if you are gentle," said Dad. "Watch out, even tiny claws can pinch!"
When he had shown the boys, Dad put the crab back where he found it. It scuttled under a big stone.

As they walked back along the beach, the children were attacked by a big swarm of flies. "The flies lay their eggs in the seaweed," said Paula.
"But they love to suck blood from bigger animals like us. Run for it!"

"Thanks for showing us the rockpools," said Dan. "You never know what you'll find," said Paula. "The seashore is a habitat for so many animals." Suddenly, James shouted out, "Look! It's a seal!"
"Is that his home?" asked Dan.
"Sort of," said Paula.
"His home stretches all around the world – it's the sea!"

WRITE YOUR OWN STORY about exploring a habitat. You also could do a drawing of a habitat showing where different animals and plants live, like this picture of a beach.

Seagulls
Rabbits
Crabs
Seaweed
Fish
Razor-shells
Seals
Limpets
Starfish

Quiz

Are all living things plants or animals?

Answer on page 6

What does a lion eat? Is a lion a predator or prey?

Answer on page 8

How can we create new habitats?

Answer on page 23

What habitats are a home for these living things?

Answer on pages 12,17,18,25

Index

Photocredits

Abbreviations: l-left, r-right, b-bottom, t-top, c-centre, m-middle. All images are courtesy of Shutterstock.com except where stated. Cover, 18 — Vilainecrevette. 1, 7b, 11 — Willyam Bradberry. 2-3, 15 — SunKids. 4 — Dennis W. Donohue. 5t — Galyna Andrushko. 5m — Simon Bratt. 5b — Razmarinka. 6 — Menno Schaefer. 6bl — Kichigin. 7t — Abramov Timur. 8l — nattanan726. 8r — Eric Isselee. 9br — Subbotina Anna. 9ml — Paul Reeves Photography. 10 — Monkey Business Images. 11tr — tratong. 11br — davemhuntphotography. 12 — Jane Rix. 12br — skydie. 13 — Panu Ruangjan. 14 — LilKar. 14tl — MarkMirror. 14bl — BENCHA STEWART. 14tr — Jan Faukner. 16 — Rob Hainer. 16bl — Adam Gryko. 17 — Roger Hall. 19 — Therina Groenewald. 19br — Rich Carey.20 — MilousSK. 21tc — Maslov Dmitry. 21br — Milosz_G. 22 — Val Thoermer. 22tr — vasakkohaline. 24br — Stockbyte. 25mr — Jim Pipe. 26t — Armin Rose. 27b — Alex Frank. 30 — withGod.